Instrumentality

"Ravi Shankar's poems are immortal in the flesh, finding in the life of the mind—its interpretations, its 'instrumentality'—the surpassing, transient lyrical moment; and in the life of the world's body the permanent, unflinching presence of thought, unconfined by time or space. They are the verbal artifacts of a singular, many-sided, and distinguished consciousness."—Vijay Seshadri

"Lovers of poetry will find in Ravi Shankar's *Instrumentality* the lucky serendipity one hopes for in a new poet: an original voice. The poems take their origin as does all fine poetry, in a love of language and a metaphorical vision combined with the imperative of music. Below the shimmering surface, however, currents of Indian spirituality and western philosophy draw the reader deeper into the works - a serious dialectic playing out in the soul of a sensitive young man pondering life's mysteries, large and small. The old questions take on a freshness and interest when seen through the new eyes of a poet of such complexity. Other times, the work is more playful. Like Wallace Stevens or the metaphysical poets, his conceits sing with intelligence, wit, and the intricacies of extended metaphor. Coming away from the work, one thinks of the jewel-encrusted coat of a raja or a wizard - a pun comes to mind: Ravishing. In a long poem celebrating the launching of the space shuttle Discovery, th poet says, 'I feel as though a part of us has lifted off.' And so it is for the reader of this fine collection of poems."—Richard Harteis

"Here are poems I've not seen before. A fog lifts and Ravi Shankar gives the reader a landscape of language filled with sharp, stainless, geometric forms. There is considerable distance to travel from page to page. Even in a poem like 'Home Together' Shankar detects a vacuum in love. From a men's room to a San Francisco sunrise, Shankar emerges with a pocketful of koans reflecting the wisdom hidden in the stars."—E. Ethelbert Miller

Instrumentality

Poems by Ravi Shankar

Cherry Grove Collections

Published by Cherry Grove Collections
P.O. Box 541106
Cincinnati, OH 45254-1106

ISBN: 1932339221
LCCN: 2003111048

Poetry Editor: Kevin Walzer
Business Editor: Lori Jareo

Typeset in Bodoni Book by WordTech Communications LLC,
Cincinnati, OH

Visit us on the web at www.cherry-grove.com

Cover design by Michael Mills
Author photo by Diane Creede

Acknowledgements

Many thanks to the editors of the publications in which the following poems have appeared:

Aark Arts Review: Oracle of Insomnia
Big City Lit: Harvest, The Field on the Horizon
Blotter: Sublime in Passing
Cimarron Review: Bhaja Govindam, Verse Four
Connecticut Review: A May-December Romance, Excerpted
     from the Terrace
Crowd: Before Dreamland Burned Down in Coney Island
Cortland Review: Carousel
Descant: Passing Through, Subsequence
Ecopoetics: Recollecting Monteverde
Good Foot: War Effort
Gulf Coast: Before Sunrise, San Francisco
The Indiana Review: Instrumentality
LIT: Paleontology's End, One Stone to Samadhi
The Massachusetts Review: Return to Mumbai
The Mississippi Review: Home Together
New Millennium: Misty Blue
Paris/Atlantic: Nocturne
The Paris Review: Blotched in Transmission, Spangling the Sea,
     Fabricating Astrology
Permafrost: Night at the Remedy
Phylum Press: Contraction
Second Avenue: Landscape in Chelsea
Six Seasons Review: Possessions
Three Point Seven: How the Search Ended
Western Humanities Review: Thought at Night, In Illinois, An Affair
Word for Word: Symbiosis, Marine Pastel

Thanks to Columbia University, the Atlantic Center for the Arts, the Ragdale Foundation and the MacDowell Colony where many of these poems took shape.

Thanks also to the following people without whose kind guidance and perceptive companionship over the years, this manuscript would not have been possible: Jon Loomis, Lisa Russ Spaar, Charles Wright, Rita Dove, Tan Lin, Melissa Kirsch, the TJ, UVA, and 2412 crew, Alfred Corn, Richard Howard, Lucie Brock-Broido, Mark Edmundson, Marie Howe, Mary Jo Salter, Alice Quinn, Marie Ponsot, Jack Hawley, Marilyn Abildskov, Sonya Sklaroff, Terri Witek, Hart Crane, Nathalie Handal, Tina Chang, Michael Mills, Rafiq Kathwari, Lee Jesse Schweppe, Sean Hahn, Jenna Kalinsky, Lexi Rudnitsky, Neil Azevedo, Cliff Weinstein, Richard Matthews, Paul Stephens, Tom Healy, Ryan Murphy, Rodney Harder, Ram Devineni, Kadam Morton Clausen, Gerhard Richter, Geri Radacsi, Mary-Lou Devine, Richard Deming, Nancy Kuhl, Mary Posner, Richard Harteis, Vivian Shipley, Gray Jacobik, Tom Hazuka, David Cappella, Steve Ostrowski, Leslie McGrath, George Bradley, the Brickwalk Poets, and to all the others off whom I've glanced, however briefly.

Finally, thanks to my parents, Rajee and K.H., sisters Rajni and Rahini, brother-in-law Ben, and nephew Valen, as well as my extended family around the world, for supporting me unconditionally through multitudinous incarnation, and thanks to Diane for providing constancy, love, and understanding even when I least deserved it. You are all, to misquote Coleridge, leading Love-throbs in my Heart.

—

Contents

I.

II.

III.

I.

The Condition of Certain Evenings

Have you noticed it? In a tower
On a depilated hillside, bells clap.
Arrival's color has faded from the sky,
Snow spreads its blanket on gray mountains.

Elsewhere, lights go on and off in cities,
Avenues clad in shadow's apparel.
Breaths go in and out of many lungs.
One by one, we wait.

Fabricating Astrology

I lie on my back in the damp grass,
Staring at the stars' mineral precision.
Masses of gas, bearers of dead light,
Mysteries snared by unreachable lairs,

How many pairs of eyes have swilled
From your glass and grown thirstier?
Will our progeny decode your songs?
My heart gives its usual answer: thrum.

The longer I gape, the more the many
Nebulae appear latticed, like a screen
In windows or a page of graph paper,
Ordered as the placement of fibulas

In feet. The chart seems plotted
Along three axes: love, labor, time.
Besotted hours converge into minus,
Kind and curative movements belong

To plus, and mirrored, both data-sets
Verge towards an identical asymptote,
Death, Provider of cardinal boundary,
Maker of the silence shapes merge with

Eventually. This much is certain:
Today I'm a day closer to extinction.
Hearse-curtains have been drawn
In every city while the stars remain

Anchored overhead. Really they move
Towards annulment in a proof I cannot
Prove. Soon enough, pattern dissolves.
Let me replace them with these words.

One Stone to Samadhi

Back in the room, it's as if we never left:
A cone of frangipani gradually charring,
And *Clair de Lune*, overlaid with whale song,

Piping through tweeters in the background,
Plastic folding-chairs filled with disparate frames
In similar postures: back straight, palms open

Upon thighs, eyes closed, muscles relaxed,
The flicker of thought, in principle, sacrificed
To the rising and falling of breath. Still a fleck

Of peripheral self can't help but remain, temporarily
Unhooked from memory's flux and grapple,
Yet attendant in some form nonetheless,

A watchfulness impartial to inclination,
Though to speak of it is like pointing a finger
At the moon. Suffice it to say that, eyes closed,

The crest on passing time's ongoing wave
Perpetually furnishes the mind with vista,
And back in the room, it's as if we never arrived

In Illinois

For Sonya Sklaroff

The way was through the lawns and past the purr
Of luxury sedans turning into
Driveways gated by electronic eyes

And marble beasts. You spoke of how light steals
Away each dawn which compels the brush
To sweep hue across the canvas, not to distill

The moment's sky—it has already forgotten
How to look—but rather, to satisfy
Some twinge, the reason why you wake

At five each morning to paint. Overhearing
Two mothers debate the merits of cash-
Mere versus the pragmatism of wool,

We concluded that these suburbs were so safe
They were lethal. And then conversation
Stopped; looming into the fog, without

An ocean's roar or salty slap, and down
A forested precipice was Lake Michigan:
Vast, imbued and unfathomable.

Blotched in Transmission

Bark of the birch, aria of the oriole, grit of the sand-grain,
In the first stanza I shall attempt to confiscate your essence
And each time, you will slip through the noose of language,
Having no owner. Your brief appearance, though, is enough
For the covetous page, conferring the illusion of presence.

Even the breaths heaving in my chest do not belong to me,
These wires of muscles tapping the hand's opposable thumb
Upon the spacebar, and the precise machinery of two pupils
Taking it in are not mine, though convenient to think so.
In the second stanza, I shall feel like an outsider in my body.

Emptied of the need to own, I become the pit of a plum.
We color our language, Wallace Stevens wrote to Elsie Moll,
And Truth, being white, becomes blotched in transmission.
In the third, final stanza, I will understand what he meant
For a moment, before the old words come flooding back.

Shapes in the Wilderness

Beneath, beyond, away, other than,
The *are* who we are happens contrapuntally
To the observation of the *are* being.
Say you and I are flashlights that shining
Out from a clearing into the forest
Shape the forest, providing trees leaves,
Mulch moisture, vivifying what world
Would fit the light of our partial rounds.
Dense, multifarious, the dark wood
Has no essence but in fleeting swaths
Of light that in illumination, define.
The fact of the flashlight, battery and bulb,
Are the only *a priories* in existence,
Though we cannot know their constituency,
Being their constituency.

Spangling the Sea

Ruffle and tuck, river fabric wags doggedly towards ocean,
Heaping surface on surface, its cadence a gown.

Perpetually beneath lurks stillness, a calm inseam sewn
By handless needles, distinct from yet part of the sequined

Design that glints iridescent now, then dark as pine.
Between silt and waver live many denizens of the deep:

Zigzagging shiners, freshwater drums, tessellated darters,
Grass carp, a kaleidoscopic plenitude that yaws and rolls

Among root wads and bubble curtains drawn on riparian
Terraces, hinged vertebrae whipping back and forth

In an elastic continuum displacing the fluid milieu,
Enabling them, polarized or not, to scull along in schools.

Nothing in outer space so bizarre as episodes underwater:
The gilled emerge from bouts of massive oviparity

Staged upon plankton columns where some fry turn larval
While the majority never leave the sure rot of egg sleep.

Whether due to snowmelt in mountainous headwater tracts
Or to rainfall from cumulonimbus fancy, for whatever reason

Water appears from serpentine soil and prairie-scrub mosaic,
A small muddy trickle that gains momentum as it swells

And deepens, sweeping along twigs, carcasses, bald tires,
To empty at length into estuaries engulfed by tides

Perpetually born of a body dressed in hastening garb,
Upholstering two-thirds more surface than any ground.

Paleontology's End

Sifting through teeth and carapaces
With a magnifying glass, you adopt
An hyperopic perspective, history
Fermenting from what continually
Ends to replenish itself. A peregrine
Falcon's scapular is slowly eaten
By soil from which poke the spoke-
Heads of late summer's dandelions
Ten thousand years later. Permian,
Ordovician, Cretaceous, Devonian,
Triassic: we've named the major
Eras of mass extinction. The past,
Happening, has preserved its portion
In amber, in crenellated clamshells
And tree bark, to augur what we'll be
For posterity. Drop the horsehair
Brush, permit the slides to drowse
In disinfectant, leave the bones;
Someone warm lies waiting.

Union

The clearing in the hills entreats
Empty rapture, shepherding hours'
Stray flocks until nothing bleats
Under the skies; insures the dower
Left for us will never cease to remain
Itself if only we proceed by twos
Into duration—spiky vervain
Is ubiquitous regard malentendu,
Our home's away, the sun's ablaze,
The way you hold up the spheres
Forms a love opaque to paraphrase
But I'll try: we've abolished fear.

Oracle of Insomnia

Unable to sleep, I miss you
Asleep and softly illuminated
Red by the alarm clock, sheets
Shucked from your shoulders
And moving perhaps, propelled
By dream into the bed's center,
Filling the space my body would
Occupy, the clatter of midnight
In Manhattan a windowpane
Away yet drowned by the whir
Of our new standing fan. Here
Now, the dark prairie, sporadic
With the display of lightening
Bugs, seems to hold a hundred
Revelations, one of which is
Unable to sleep, I miss you.

Possessions

Blear gray expanse, medium for shrieking gulls,
Places a wreath of fog upon the dormant verbs of hulls

Conjugated by docks worn splintery and cribriform.
Gray numb expanse that today will not break into storm

According to the weather report pinned above the tide
Tables in a Marine Supply Store's window. Don't deride

The shopping opportunities at this modest, slightly unclean
Establishment: stock such as hanks of polypropylene

Rope, citronella candles, tarp holders, maps that mark
Wreck sites for divers and marlin for fisherman, shark

Tooth necklaces, tubes of mildew resistant silicone—
Stuff you never imagined you'd have a sudden desire to own.

Before Dreamland Burned Down in Coney Island

Certainly it was splendid to see you again,
The trout on your pate was quite fetching,
And I did my best impression of fulfilling
Your dream of me: skittish, acerbic, sly.

The ditch I was pitched in proved to be a parlor,
The rattling prattle of folks for whom "Callous"
Was an island in the Mediterranean.
I brought them drinks on a mirrored tray.

Along the heave of boardwalk, neon sliced
Evening into bite-size portions for squalid
Sailors and salacious pseudo-rodeo clowns.
An ebb of pleasure coterminous with despair.

And soon, as before, the wheel in the sky
Turned, my ear got caught on rope spoken
Through the barker's mouth while metal bottles
Toppled. Then you stole away the fish's eye.

Passing Through

Yesterday, evening as sultry
As an exhalation,
Sky tilting against the phosphorescent
Cove of the abandoned plaza,
Yellow slipping from the knots of primrose,

I saw you
For less than thirty seconds
But that which passed between us—innocent,
Concupiscent, uncooked—was enough to skew
The orbit of whatever happened after

We went our separate ways; this morning
I woke disoriented from dream,
Knowing that because we shall meet
Never again,
You have skewered a piece of me.

Thought at Night

Nearly impossible to separate
The roof from the blacking weight
That presses in the screened-off windows
Girding the perimeter of this dusty cupola—
Every line here blurs as I chew

The insides of my chapped lips
To keep from inviting oblivion to hammer
Blood into the moment's monumental
Supremacy. The air between us dampens
Under the spokes of my unshaved face,

Lolls with the musk between your knees,
How easy it would be...
Surrounded on all sides by obscurity
And not grace—you build nests
While words fly from my mouth like terns

Plunging for prey iridescent beneath
The surf—since talking to you I am thinking
Of betraying her, a thousand miles removed
From our conversation about truth
In lending, a banking term for laying

All your cards out face-up (the gaming
Metaphor for the absence of games),
Though the way you say it,
It seems to mean how we extend
Credit to each other, loaning our bodies

On security, hoping to accrue
The greatest possible interest right now
Not so much as later. The way you say it,
I understand all relationships
Are about exchange. Standing with my arms

Crossed behind my back, I stare
At the great nothing of the roof and the trees,
Slowly taking shape in the greater nothing
Of night, wondering what to do with the dark
Realization that I don't belong to myself.

A May-December Romance

Wide, woven, the brim of a straw hat shades
Her eyes as she leans against a stack of crates,
The dock buzzing with arrival and departure.

She holds in one hand a bouquet of nosegays,
Straightens the other arm as if to feed a gull.
The speck of his ship has long since vanished

And now sunlight glances off a barge's prow,
Reveals again a shopworn tale. Deeply, she inhales.
Everything is predestined in retrospect.

A fisherman lugs a tub of ice onto a lanyard deck.
The wind stirs an abandoned hank of rope,
Lifts her linen dress until it reveals red kneecaps.

What was the last thing he murmured to her?
She remembers nothing save the way
His chin, unshaven, felt against her tongue.

A clomp of boots breaks her uneven respiration.
Momentarily, she'll fling the bouquet into seas
The color of gray she has never before seen.

The Field on the Horizon

Sitting on a wooden bench, in the surround
Of foliate faces, palmettos that fantail in midair,
Shivering leaves all wrapped in the bright shroud
Of early afternoon, I'm thinking of you my dear,

And how much history we share. Here, the living
Is done in the present tense, away from city teeth,
Daily irritants, a pace that insures even lounging
Is stressful. Here, I can't help telling the truth

To everyone I meet. Yesterday we went to see
The manatees, and instead saw mounds of rubbish—
Soda cans, used oil-filters, moldy paperbacks—
And two locals casting a line into the polluted rash

Of the Intercoastal. Sure hope they don't work
At Shell's Seafood, where we ate last night.
Have you been happy? I suppose that with a wick
I've melted away what wax we had. Now with a net

The man I've almost become is going in search
Of the man it seems I'm becoming. Can we follow
Each other through these changes? Ahead, a stretch
Of loam—hard to tell if it's in bloom or fallow.

An Affair

Licorice scent: an opalescence paws
Loose the hunger, whirring intricate

Machinery into action—partitioning,
Justifying, attaching veils—as focus

Stiffens to one point of release now
And near, velvety as the underside

Of repercussion; so the kept colludes
With the keeper to obliterate itself.

Rankles

For Priscilla Becker

Bones, have you no pliancy?
Propping me up when clearly I've collapsed,
Upholding no form save desire. Listen,

All's not right with daylight. A kind of kudzu
Strangles transient hearts. The weight
Of summer has begun to drag down the fall,

Still the leaves, stubborn, cling to their stems.
The creatures who've long been stalking me
Have on their lips unpronounceable syllables

Which, if uttered, might furnish one version
Why. Not that you, skeletal fretwork, care
One whit about my predicaments. That's fine:

My vigil won't be interrupted. I'll wait here
Till this world of one becomes a world of none,
Till with osseous glee I am supplanted.

Symbiosis

One alternative to speech is wheatless streets
Where caught mid-impetus, even lampposts
Rusted cursive partake of flow:
This into that, shadow ceding mass, intake output,
Not headed anywhere particularly but particular
Nonetheless, the way the cracked curb
Appears granular in sunlight,
Both existing not from their own end
But in symphony with that which converts
Their presence into nouns, as if that fixes
Anything in place, root-sure with the necessity
Of clavicles, igneous rocks and thunderclaps.
With obstinate grace things slip name's knots.
A bright moth, lanced on pins of rhetoric,
Sloughs off tremulous meaning, even in decay,
Even under the magnifying glass' oblong eye.
Only a blossom can define proboscis.

Stillness

For K.H. Shankar

Before the advent of expectation
    Lives emptiness: distant hills blushing
        With the horizon, one b flat pulled
            Apart at song's end,
    A hush of atoms holding together a planet. Father,

Beyond plotting degree days, derivatives,
    Sums and quotients, there is vacuum,
        A certainty that we are a conductor,
            Not *the* conductor,
    For a whole far greater than its parts. Amazing

Relinquishing control. Not the path
    Of least resistance, not *a* path,
        But standing still as the sun drifts west,
            As silence shorelines
Music, as hollow particles assert hallowed architecture.

Instrumentality

For true *handschumachers*, whose numbers, thanks to machines,
Have dwindled, stitching together gloves is the highest calling.

Preferable to shearing bolts of cloth or shoeing in a tatty alley,
As the old joke goes, who ever saw anyone speak using their boots?

Glove-making is true art and hierarchical in profession as five
Fingers: silkers, closers, fourchetters, all under the thumb of cutters

Who can tell at a glance whether a cut of leather is South African
Capeskin or peccary shorn from Brazilian wild boars, whether a glove

Is sewn with half- or full-piqué stitches, its finish velvet or grain.
Such depths of knowing exist in the performance of any occupation

From learning how to hold a rattan and rubber marimba mallet
To memorizing the occult order of four cylinders and sixteen valves.

Even communication is apprenticeship in hue and nuance,
Threads garlands of articulated sound to festoon upon toolcraft:

Praise the intervention of utensils for extending person into matter!
Praise the crows, levers, handspikes, pinions, cranks, winches,

Cams, pedals, wedges, screws, heddles, wheels, planes, springs,
Latches, keys that provide attention a momentary respite from itself,

Because in fleeting occupation, even the most dogged ego dissolves.
The diffusion of personality via tools is grace, so grace to the fingers

Of the pastry chef who kneads dough into flour and grace to the flags
The air-traffic controller whisks through the runway's turbulent air,

Grace for all task which focuses notice to the eviction of doubt,
Leaving action's unstuttering arc, which is eloquence and muteness

At once, to turn the bars of time into a provisional, shoreless field.
I want to live where glove-makers are singular artificers in the world

In which their pliers ply. I'll swap you my head for a stabbing awl.
Remember when the first basalt flakes were chipped from boulders

To make hand-axes that could dismember most carcasses the
          hominid
We once were might have hunted down? The moment when the words

Sunder and *salmonella* entered the language? Was it corporeal act
Before idea, disembodied before uttered as sound? Did the
          Triangulum

Have a pinwheel before we a telescope? That's koan, unanswerable–
Better to lay eyeglasses at Hephaestus' forge as alms for the
          prosthetics

Which grant our bodies metaphors for itself. Because before the
          invention
Of the pump, there was one less way to understand the human heart.

II.

Before Sunrise, San Francisco

Bruno's by sallow candlelight,
The jacketed barkeep counting
Tips from a jam jar and horseshoe
Booths burnished a bit too bright,

Yet the stained mahogany walls
And the lazy lament of Spanish
Horns from speakers huddled
In the corner speak a different

Language altogether, one that rolls
Effortlessly off the tongue and fills
The room like myrrh, a promise sent
That four walls can indeed keep out

The world, that when horns wail
For percussion and those walls
Are elegantly attired, why there
Is no need to ponder the gristle

In the Mission outside, no need
To wonder why that one left you
Or why you are always too
Late. The weight of your existence

Roughly equals the martini glass
In front of you, the thick mass
Of the past collapses into brightness
As well-lit as the dripping star

At the center of your table.
Nod. Snap your fingers. Order
Another drink. Let horns grieve,
Let the wristwatch think on sheep

Before you leave. Tonight,
The only eyes on you are two
Pimentos stuffed into olives
Bloated with vermouth and gin.

Whistle

Having dispatched to the world replicas,
The man in the middle of sundry moods
Rescinded—was it too late?—and aimed

At gathering in specks of lapsed hours,
Snippets of behavior that left him feeling
Alone exiled from grace. No bones.

Each act, once acted, was irrevocable,
Another verse in the Bible of nothingness
Between whose covers his days would run.

Night at The Remedy

Seated on the arm that extends
Tattered from the couch, you glow
In the bar's low light, moored amid
Cracked peanut shells, empty ashtrays,
The drunken roar of fraternal glee
That surrounds us. You tell me how
A friend believes that by bedding
Innumerable women, he attains the spirit
Of one, holding fragments to his chest
Until it begins to feel like his mother.

Your knee is very close to mine.
And I am reminded of the study
Concluding perfect beauty was made
By superimposing face on face
On face ad infinitum till the gestalt
Emerged, vacant and symmetric.
You tremble with what you brought
Through the darkened entrance;
My vision distorts in this gray air.
I want to peer into another as much

As anyone but knowing most views
Hurt, I defer. You speak of veering
Off every path into interim abodes,
That eventually you'll arrive full-circle.
Perhaps you will. No one has put
A song on, and balls knock together
On red felt behind us. Two minutes
Until midnight, two pints of bitter—
What wouldn't happen if we touched?

Thalassic Hour

Pitched from sleep's bareback steed,
My reflection confronts me in the mirror:
No glory in the bundle of gaunt features,
No escape from narrow, furrowed eyes.
Many times, in vain, I've tried to lead
Him across the ford where bumblebees
Fit their hairy orbs to honeycomb
And tawny-armed kin play the tambour
After weeks tilling fields of cane.
Under a sickle moon's sharpened rim,
Downpour broods. Still, he transfixes me:
In the corner, where mirror and frame
Converge, a minute, black-sailed ship
Has begun its long journey towards him.

Returning from Hell's Kitchen

Now that the gargoyles have oxidized,
Skyscraper stalks sprout lenticular panes.
Another rush-hour overpowers the hush
Or such ambient din as passes for silence
In the self-proclaimed center of the world.

Underground, trains groan into stations
To be filled with eyes that never marry,
Toothless mouths that occasionally break
Into songs about joy in the face of loss,
The rhythm section a few coins in a cup,

The rest all pleats and loosened ties,
Various gears unscrewed from labor's
Leviathan watch. Simple not to muse
When in transit: people board, disembark,
And instantly, the space they leave is filled.

Sublime in Passing

After Raymond Chandler

Carbonated gurgle of seltzer,
Dishrag snap inside the abscess
Of each pilsner glass, the barkeep's
Broken whistle as he folds napkins
Into triangles—such subtle ado
Resolves into bergs of anticipation
As night shatters serenity, draws us in,
Erratic as meteors. I order a scotch
On stones, slouch towards sloppy
Jabber down the rail: one a few stops
Short of lit cradling his boilermaker
As if sprouted from the wooden stool.

Then you step in.

It's as though someone in back yanked
The emergency brake on the joint, lurching
The hum to a halt. The barman hangs
In mid-polish, the drunk swivels
Without swallowing, spittle dribbling
Down-chin, and for a flash, all sounds
Ebb, as when a conductor skims a gaze
Across the pit, taps on the music stand,
And holds two hands poised in the air—
So I sit wide-eyed, holding in breath.
It's not until you famously take a booth
That the dive once again expands.

Landscape in Chelsea

Garbled gray, the lean beaked bird aquiver upon the post
With needle eyes discerns bulldozers regurgitating silt,
Cataracts of people edging past an orange-vested man
Fronting a quarry noisily being turned into a Multiplex.

One by one hoary sites are razed to raise new steel girders,
Leaving traffic with less lanes and more honking rancor
Sporadically nonstop. Scraped billboard flakes overflow
The gutters, the latest face stretches glossily along buses,

Men wearing hypo-allergenic masks emerge from grates
That lead beneath the sidewalks to where waste resides,
While on a block hung with plastic sheets, steam machines
Whine ear-splitting fumes to beat dust from damp walls.

The city, never to be finished, juxtaposed with a pigeon,
Eternally recurrent, hints at an address that I, being a bit
Of neither and a bit of both, yet something else besides,
Can neither decipher nor disregard as the light changes

And sundry vehicles pause in phalanx at the crosswalk,
Perpendicularly retrograde to the surge of pedestrians
With whom, under pigeon-gray skies, I am swept along
In dissonant, improvisational song. All of history is here

Now, and the city, our protean home, is a confabulation
In the minds of those who have yet to be born. Gods
Are swept up by the street cleaners on alternate days,
While through clots of diesel soot, gray birds still skate.

How the Search Ended

Before the bus flattened me,
I was searching for a scent
Never to be remembered
Until it was smelled again.

My fault not the driver's:
I had stopped to stare at a girl
Undressing in her window.
I was too far to smell her.

Earlier, I had visited a palm reader,
Not to trace my lifeline, merely
To discover where to buy
An oversize neon hand.

On the way home, my head jangled
With a premise: Life is either more or less
Serious than I imagine it to be.
And then came the bus.

A Story with Sand

After James Dickey's *A Birth*

Inventing a story with sand,
I find gray anklebones broken
By the shore and not a horse
To graze upon my sand.

Better off. I haven't a lasso
And my trousers are too tight.
Like one side of a medallion
The sand clarifies the point

That these lines cannot hold.
Afternoon beats its tom-tom.
The shore gathers gull-cries.
Contingency is the new god.

Not an umbrella on the beach.
Wheels of clouds cross the sky.
That that happened, this does.
Mouths murmur ears of shale.

Waves came to the shore.
From before came the sand .
The sand lacked a horse.
Afternoon held no plan.

Driftwood sprains the shore.
You had to be here for this.
We could have been different
But past shapes still remain.

Driftwood and anklebones.
Afternoon beats its tom-tom.
Not an umbrella on the beach.
Elsewhere horses ruminate.

Shaking Free of Epiphany

Remember that voice which briefly nested
In your friend's mouth as you both stood
On a mountaintop fringed with trillium

Wondering what to do with the rest of life,
A runnel of wind winding through the trees?
Remember how the voice, which was not

Quite your friend's voice, being somehow
Deeper, more pronounced and bell-like,
Bypassed the usual interpretive mechanisms,

Spoke directly to your constitutional core?
Remember the memories that surged up then,
Of being a child in a clearing gazing at stars

Bare arms infused with the crispness of grass,
The steady whine of crickets scoring the dark,
Every element, including yourself, pristine?

That was when, though later you'd disavow it,
Tears came, along with a need for something
You might, if you weren't so modern call

Redemption, a poignant awareness of how
Far from the child you'd been you'd come
And how much farther there was to go,

The only guide to what lay ahead threadbare
Words that had been spoken too many times
By too many people to hold significance.

Where on the horizon were the new words,
The ones the size of pills, the color of plums,
Sharpened and stainless as geometric forms,

The words that curled the toes in convulsion,
Stole behind the barn with a can of gasoline
And lit a match, danced round the flames

So as to summon drought from the rains?
Where were the words that would transform
Facsimile folk, turning slurs pure as spring

Water, saturating pores of Diaspora,
Words that would partake equally of neon
And oak leaf, timeless yet encompassing

The prefixes neo-, hyper-, cyber- and post-,
Where on the tip of your tongue were they?
The wind then, not in response, eddied

Through the green scrim of birch and ash,
And a white-tailed deer sprang in front of you,
Rubbing its nose against the ground, casting,

If demeanor can be imputed to animals,
A prolonged, quizzical glance at the two of you
Before bounding into the leaf-heavy beyond.

When you turned to your friend to confirm
The passing creature, no sounds would come
From your mouth, though ideas teemed;

Somehow the self at the helm of the larynx
Was estranged from the one picking wordless
Fruit on the shores of intention. A disconnect.

Have you forgotten what happened next,
How in your friend's eyes, which until now
Had resembled noon-light refracted through

A magnifying glass, personality was restored,
The bell-like voice replaced by familiar
Intonations, the parasite returned to its host?

How you put your arms around each other
As if having survived an infantry's final burst?
How the clear skies broke into storm,

A hard rain buffeting briefly then dying out?
The car ride down the mountain was filled
With silence, both of you turning over coins

Of thought minted in different countries,
Unable to explain to each other a hairline
Fracture appearing in your sense of things,

An imperative indelibly etched on any plans
You might make in the near or far,
And so you listened instead to indie rock

Crackling through the car speakers, watched
The onset of evening through the windshield,
Patches of mailbox-fronted homes scrolling past.

That night, alone, the blue light of television
Could not diminish your neural circuitry's buzz,
Your palpable certainty that ontological

Change was fermenting in your chest, that
You could engage the real as the deer did,
Regal and unwavering in pursuit of finality.

That night you dreamed of a black hull nudging
Past silt and reeds, opening into an expanse
Of flawless rippling ocean, interstitial spaces

Shifting while maintaining a pattern between
The wingtips of gulls wheeling in formation
Overhead, skies roughly the color of the sea,

A gray blanket of serenity that swaddled you . . .
If only morning hadn't come, but it did,
Refastening hasps on an extant worldview,

The thought processes which conveyed you
From fast-food lunches to movie houses,
From facing mirrors to the back of bars,

Though you were never quite able to forget
What transpired that day on the mountaintop.
O parched, membranous glutton! How many

Years have passed since you first saw the light
Gleaming from the mask of your friend's face
Who is now married, expecting a third child?

How many years paralyzed, unable to decipher,
Have you tried to love someone who loves you
But found it nearly impossible to do so?

"You remember too much," a toothless sibyl
Diagnosed, "your corolla has been tinged black
By a curse put on you in some former life."

She gave you crystals to dissolve in a hot bath,
Lotion made from an extract of bergamot
And vetiver root, three beeswax candles to light

At the stroke of midnight, but it hasn't helped,
Has it? My advice to you—beware, it's biased—
Is to sit on a mat that vibrates at eight thousand

Angstroms and concentrate on a plastic ashtray,
Lime-green and perfect in its Platonic oval,
And if that fails, to pick up a pencil and write.

III.

Return to Mumbai

Bombay no longer, the island
Circumscribed by water exhausts
Herself in rain. For six months,

Her suitors, Vasai, Ulhas, Thane,
Spar, each swelling, vigorously
Surging, empurpling against

The horizon's taut washboard.
She, placid, stares breathless,
Smiles the smile of a schoolgirl

Whose step-father has just left
For London and decidedly opens
To each. Already, her soil soaks.

Already she sings in preparation,
Rust-colored flames smoldering
Compost, plastic tarps flapping,

Held down by planks, stones,
Discarded tires; dirt roads gravid
With rickshaws, vegetable wallahs

Whipping bullocks, Tata trucks
Distended with diesel, yellow
And black taxis like so many drones

Evacuating the hive, bicycles,
Ambassadors, Maruti Suzikis,
Creaking double decker buses

Emblazoned with the latest
Bollywood star, women in fraying
Saris, barefoot men collecting

Alms, children praying, their shape
More rail than real. From an island
Mother, rising water fathers

This mitotic *bharathanatyam*,
An embryonic dance held
Until the obstetrician's arrival.

Men's Room

Cuffs rolled, wing tipped, a torso-less spook sits
Immune, encased behind a roughcast wall
And plastic doors latched by a pin of steel.
The polygonal floor below has turned

To grimy signatures of sneaker tread
That ammonia-doused, a mop could not remove.
Beside the sink a growth of sodden forms—
A pulpy mass of gum and paper towels—

Irradiate the white fluorescent buzz
That imitates mosquitoes overhead.
The spook, unseen, in silence holds a grunt
Within his cheeks until I turn to leave.

When I return there's water on the mirror.
A curl of hair stuck to the porcelain sink.
Dear sir you left a smell and a scintilla
Of piss upon a seat that wasn't raised.

The Flock's Reply to the Passionate Shepherd
After Christopher Marlowe

Marooned upon this grassy knoll,
We wander lost from vale to pole,
Our wooly backs resemble thorn,
It's been a while since we've been shorn.

You waste much time trying to woo
That nymph who never will see you.
Since it's a shepherd that you are,
You're better off courting a star.

But over here, your loyal flock
Needs no clasp, no precious rock
To follow you from field to field:
If love's your need, we can but yield.

Have you not heard us cry and bleat
When you approach us, then retreat?
We miss your orders and your laugh,
We even miss your clouting staff.

Save those gowns made of our wool,
No need to make belts or to pull
Posies from the hillside's crease—
That nymph is what we call a tease.

Just as the hours wing away,
There are some sheep that love to play:
If such delights your mind might move
Then live with us and be our love.

Excerpted from the Terrace

Last night we gathered
In dilapidated chairs to prattle
Over water's slow burble
Into the fountain, each of us
Moistened with pinot grigio,
Woozy enough to believe
We could not only be artists
But make a difference
In our respective medium—
The painter spoke of edges
Mediating a conversation
Between opacity and depth;
The composer raised a toast
To heterophonia, to being
Out of phase; the graphic
Designer complained
That everywhere she looked
She saw herself,
Not a smarmy, arrogant thought,
But genuine bewilderment
At the nature of coincidence,
How material objects hold
The power to resonate
Days later as if someone
Was always watching,
And then all discussion
Ended. We each watched
The last flecks of amber
Slowly abolish the horizon,
Or listened to the water,
Or retreated into the dark grottos
Behind our eyelids

Before someone noticed the lull
And commented upon it,
Saying pauses happened
Every twenty minutes,
That was when the angels passed,
And so conversation resumed,
Though the poet remained silent,
Wondering whether we impose
Or extract meaning from the unfolding
Into our hours,
And whether it makes a difference.

Clearing the Way

Yesterday, when each thought stalled at the tracks
Crossing the possible, I borrowed oil
Paints and corkboard, hoping to daub away

Encumbrance. Window-framed, the prairie stretching
Wild grass (bluestem spoked with blazing-star)
To the horizon was foregrounded by many

A limbed hickory, and deigned the occasional
Illumination by some cloud-evading rays.
A perfect subject for illustration.

Squirting pigment—knolls of cadmium
Red and viridian, great smears of rose
Madder, no more than a splotch of burnt

Umber—on wax-paper, I began,
With tentative strokes, an attempt to extract
The hour's passing. Suffice it to say,

Whatever respect I had for painters
Has since exponentially increased.
Confounded by how to reach the edges

Of the canvas, lacking perspective or balance,
I was unable to communicate hand-
To-brush and the intended landscape, roosting

Precariously on my slanted desk, began
To transform: the grasses became a school
For disabled paisley, the hickory

Metamorphosed into a skirted stick-
Woman, the sky turned into a swampy
Impasto and the result was somewhere

Between impressionism and expressionism,
A garish, well-composed, masterpiece
Of oppressionism, school of affront

To the sense of sight. Today I am still
Scrubbing paint-chips from the desktop
And out of my scalp. The painting, dried,

Lies upside down on the radiator, serving
Well its intent; I need only to look over
For a reminder of why I choose to write.

Marine Pastel

Chromatic waves of sound wash vibrations into inlets,
Shape the place bacteria emerges from with unasked
Pressure merging atoms into and out of ionic bonds
So that microscopic life can develop from tidewater,

Disputing entropy by growing more complex in time:
Voices from an ocean teeming speak shells into spirals
That spell chaos, brackish and baroque, unpredictable.
Formed by weather, more habitual in retrospect

When limned in crystal or decomposing underground, nature
Is *in medias res* forever, temporarily inhabiting a succession
Of forms: watery squiggles, phosphoric roots, magma-
Parched craters that distill briefly into veins of thought.

Discovery Suite

1.

Sibilant static pierces the dream,
Punctures the hour with a needle
    Of wakefulness. A spectral room
Holds the receipt for dawn's bid,
    Grayness pries through the blinds,
Somewhere ospreys warble,
    And from bed to stumble, I land
Groggily under a spew
    Of hot water. Today's exceptional,
The chance for a launch,
    If no systems-components stall,
The *Discovery* will ember, punch out
    Of the Earth's vast atmosphere,
Bound for numb, lifeless recesses
    In outer space. Imagine the fear,
The thrill of the seven astronauts
    Waiting for the word in white suits,
Their capsule filled with sensors,
    Freeze-dried meals, moon boots,
And cases of avionics equipment.
    Tomorrow they'll see our planet
Rising, like a sun, from a porthole
    In the command module. Not yet.
Now they're considering the ground.

2.

"Fifteen seconds," announces a retiree with an azure
fanny pack and earphones clamped around her head.

On a wooden lookout at Canaveral National Seashore,
The Atlantic Ocean breathing spumes flecked pinkish

By the sun, rows of sedge creating chiaroscuro effect
Against the sand, we stand. Each of us is the still center

Of our own universe, holding our breaths in anticipation.
"Ten seconds," she declares. The voice of an impresario.

"Nine—eight—seven," the countdown winding down.
None of us quite sure where to look or what to look for.

Three pelicans, in a line, beaks to the surface of the sea,
Wings outspread, look for wriggling things to snap up.

"Three—Two—One!" Then, nothing. Pellucid waves
Continue, dispassionately, to break against the beach

As feet shift and someone sharply intakes their breath.
Then, miles beyond reach, a smudge of smoke follows

An extended jag of orange, like a flare's ignited edge.
That's it! Rising systematically on a pillar of propulsion,

A coruscating interloper in the bright morning skies,
The *Discovery*, carrying aloft the *Starshine*, a small satellite,

Arcs elegantly upwards, turning with the Earth's orbit
So that eventually it will gain enough speed to tear free

Of her hold and enter the cosmos. We, silent, track
The ascending orange scar until it heals to a whiter fleck.

And soon, a binocular-toting tourist proclaims the booster-
Rockets have been released, and though it's too hard

For me too see, I murmur my approval. The shuttle grows
Ever smaller, merging finally with the sprawl of clouds,

And still it's there, barely visible, scaling a predestined
Trajectory, heading to dock at the Space Station

Where teams of specialists are studying gravity.
I watch intently until my eyes can no longer focus,

And even then, I still feel the launch in my stomach,
Somehow made complicit in the highest of human

Endeavors. Only after we resume our familiar poses
Do we hear the rumble and pop of the passed event,

Sound having taken longer to crawl upon the beach.
We listen. Then someone asks a question, is answered.

A boy plunges into the surf. Identities begin to return.
As we turn to the van on Turtle Mound Road, I linger

To absorb the wake: vapor trail disappearing, vibrations
Like a cough. I feel as though a part of us has lifted off.

Subsequence

For Marilyn Abildskov

A day has passed since we loaded
Boxes distended with impressions
Jotted years ago in journals, books
Unread, whatever charms a writer
Needs to keep (mere guesses now;
Those boxes were heavy) going
At, after all's been said, a torturous
And remarkable calling, back into

The Toyota Tercel you drove here
From Iowa. One day and I'll have
You know, I slept like lumber last
Night, had trouble reviving myself
This morning from the bituminous
Anesthetic of vacancy. Now I share
The porch with a graphic designer,
With whom I'll exchange hundreds

Of silences each day, stepping out
Only for one of my two daily
Cigarettes and, perhaps, to caress
The foil neck, risen from a brown
Paper bag, of the nasal decongestant
Of a red wine you left behind.
The night before you quit, I imagine
Our souls ascended like smoke

Above a patch of burning prairie,
Forcing me to acknowledge how
The edges of events are blunted
In memory, given false body

In speech, set off, in the mind,
From a larger whole that sums
All action; I was wielding willful
Deceit, no match for your acuity,

And if you believe people can be
Vehicles for someone else's truth,
Then you were one. Clarity came
The next morning at autonomy's
Expense, but so it goes, what's lost
Gets gained another way—advice
A man with dark eyes and dark hair
Was prophesied to give. Those words

Are write on, and perhaps someday
We'll manage to share a pedestrian
Moment together, supine in a blaze
Of corn under a frothy moon
We shall reminisce and continue
Old arguments—debating aesthetics
Of loss versus the lost aesthetics—
Or just lay gazing up, doing nothing.

Contraction

Honest self-scrutiny too easily mutinies,
    mutates into false memories
Which find language a receptive host,
Boosted by boastful embellishments.

Self-esteem is raised on wobbly beams,
    seeming seen as stuff enough
To fund the hedge of personality,
Though personally, I cannot forget

Whom I have met and somehow wronged,
    wrung for a jot of fugitive juice,
Trading some ruse for a blot or two,
Labored to braid from transparent diction

Fiction, quick fix, quixotic fixation.
    As the pulse of impulses
Drained through my veins, I tried to live
Twenty lives at once. Now one is plenty.

Sunset over Morningside Park

How attribute the flux of thought to stuff
Made from the join and part of molecules
As easily seen as the incessant sough
Of evening wind blown to forestall the duel
Between the last of light and start of dusk,
The victor guaranteed a daily loss
While worlds lay caught within the brusque
Expanse of dream we regularly fly across,
Deaf to the sound of our extrinsic bounds
Breaking into knowledge of who's been born
From broth: an antecedent never to be found.
Light passes; the moment's notice is shorn
   Of guise because it cannot give of null.
   Seems like it might have been a miracle.

Nocturne

For Barbara Scheggia

Barbara, once you bisected your name
For me, traced *Barb* back to its scabrous
Origin: dark continents, bearded men,

Unheard shrieks, the necessary estate
Of caustic heredity. Your face, my dear,
Hangs sporadically over my bed, a moon

Gone gibbous, rung in sanguine wreaths
Where from newly mortared chests
Twilight heaps veins atop evergreen eyes

That suture mine to non-pacific prophecy:
Comets reared from craters, coastlines
In fierce kiss after placid aeons, shards

Of beer bottle arranged upon porcelain
Set with silver cutlery on fretted tablecloth,
The unlit face that lingers in vanity mirrors,

All specters that have much more to do
With me—curled, unable to look away—
I know than you. Even fictive, you flee.

Picasso once wrote, *On tue ce qu'on aime*,
And indeed to possess is to destroy,
Maxim for each bouncing baby broken

From the womb. Yet how to extinguish
Ownerless flames that burn my bed
Between cement walls and fetid gullies?

Rather I'll clutch gauze-white sheets, long
For overpowering sleep: every summit
Erodes enfin and most ditches are filled.

War Effort

Months after bombs reminded the town
Of the countryside that it'd been built on,
There are still some green patches,
And when it rains, a crocus or two
Fleetingly nudge purple heads into bloom.

If the landscape retains the memory
Of those who lived their lives in it,
It chooses not to disclose such details—
No scrap of garment nor rusted barrow
Nor spinal column remains.

These days the sun continues to shine,
Ants parade in lines, the wind wheezes,
And on the remnants of a dusty road
That once held hospitals,
Prowls a mongrel in search of its leash.

Incantation

O haruspex! Sift through your mother's viscera,
Untangle her entrails to find in that first home
Evidence of a final one fitter than a womb,
A plot unfathomable as shovels full of loam.
O thaumaturge!
           Yoke this line periodic to the sun
So that, soaring, it discerns a fall (it will fall),
And falling discerns it does not move at all.
In the ocean, the horizon bobs and fluctuates
With a whale's fluke while above iris swells
A gull's beak plucks parallax from two blue hands.
Nothing ever disbands. The thought then arises
That thoughts arising unbidden are yours
No more than bracken bracketing a fen is mine.

Harvest

Remembering the day we met
I cannot remember our attire
Or on what we so easily spoke,
Any trace remains transformed,
Gone as bulbs, once marigolds
Take shape. Phosphorescent
Along the mattress on the floor,
What exactly didn't we know
About pain? The garden grown
Abundant between us was orb-
Lit in secret. We couldn't share
What ripened with anyone else.

Carousel

Singeing the heels of a quarrel,
Another renewal, with what for fuel?

Is it courage or fear that brings us
Both tears, each unable to leave the other?

Outside, the world displays its devices,
Lures and entices, promises pleasures

Earnest as arsenic and easier than rain.
Which must be why we refrain . . . It's true,

That with you I'm shriven, but remember
When we were children, and joy

Joy was a given.

Home Together

Between us the vacuum of early evening,
A pot of rice and beans simmering on the stove.
Between us, for now, an easy domesticity,
The way we move past each other without words ,
A thin breeze hitched up to bay windows,
Our footsteps rattling on the hardwood floors.
Words are there though, invisible yet sharp
As incisors pulled from a hound's drooling jaw,
Words we can never have meant to speak,
But did, recanted, then spoke again.
Such words should have died in our lungs.
They have staked between us a fence of teeth.

Recollecting Monteverde, Costa Rica

Don't bother me.
Last week is rapidly browning;
I am trying to bring it back edgeless.
Surely I was feeling something,
Catching my breath in the cloud-forest.

Staring at that patchwork of green—
Uncurling fronds, whorled bromeliads,
Corkscrewing saplings, ferns the size
Of baby elephants, spores that carpeted
Tree limbs, lianas garroting the canopy—

Flocks of revelations must have used me
As their nest. Hemmed in by the hum
Of vast organic engines churning out life,
I remember thinking that what I liked
About forests was what I liked about the sea:

They've already been made. That's more
Innate laziness than genuine revelation:
An alembic emptying. For an afternoon,
I was perforated by the rustling of agoutis,
The swoop of daffodil-bellied oropendolas,

Electric come-hither of blue morphos,
A dormant green that on closer inspection
Showed schemes of teeming insect-life,
And now alone in a stucco room, I hunker.
Please bother me.

Double-Bind

The constant whine of lines
Has left me tired, bereft of stimulus,

Stranded at a shallow precipice
Unable to leap. Concentrate.

Bundling cognition to a point,
There's the tightened speck of it,

Empty, just redacted, tensed—
Inseparable from its container.

Bhaja Govindam Verse Four
Translated from the Sanskrit

नलिनीदलगतजलमतितरलं
तद्वज्जीवितमतिशयचपलम् ।
विद्धि व्याध्यभिमानग्रस्तं
लोकं शोकहतं च समस्तम् ॥
(भज-गोविन्दं भज-गोविन्दं....) [4]

—Sri Bhagavadpada Shankara

The water-drop trembles upon a lotus petal.
Pureed early peas dribble down my chin.
I squall. Someone reads to me, if I am
Lucky. Green turns to brown, my bare feet

Benumbed by checkerboard tile. Turns back
To green. I trade waddling for two wheels,
Using the sidewalk as starlings use the sky.
Soon my sandwiches are sealed in plastic

And I scribble sentences in spiral notebooks:
Jane *picked, picks, will pick* an apple from
The tree. When evening calls, my body listens
In spurts. Here an inch, there a curve, there

Nothing at all. I discover deodorant, discard
Tube socks, smooth my limbs or upper lips.
The world outside becomes a mirror inside
My mind. Soon I trade two wheels for four,

Speed to the shore with windows down, beer
Chilling in the trunk, my hand on someone's
Thigh. Waves crash, recede, splinter into foam.
The sun slinks from the sky. All the cheering

Stops. Suddenly I find myself collating
Or married and hating what I do each day.
I spend my paychecks on color televisions
With surround sound, drink two scotches

For lunch, sleep with that stranger down
The block to compensate, I tell myself,
To inject some thrill into this farm animal
Of a life. When the kids appear, my brow

Has the permanent etching of a cenotaph,
Parenting scars. Love habituates, the kids
Bluster about independence, the will wears
Into reflex and the vacations are not enough.

In time retired, house vacated, I stir to strap
A camera around my neck as accompaniment
To the ubiquitous sweat-shirt, securing
A constant peregrination berth, spouting

From *Jet d'eau* to *Fontana di Trevi*, yet life
Remains as unstable as passage across sea.
Possibly my heart fails or kidneys mutiny
Or I am flapjacked by a French *malfaiteur*

In a humpback Citroen. Kids may bring
Carnations through rollaway cloth curtains
Smelling of disinfectant. Perhaps then,
With sustenance and spilth cathetered,

I will see my life, family, fellow citizens,
This planet Earth suspended in an amplitude
Of stars, as a single water-drop loosed from
A lotus petal, spreading drowsy circles in a lake.

Exile

There's nowhere else I'd rather not be than here,
But here I am nonetheless, dispossessed,
Though not quite, because I never owned
What's been taken from me, never have belonged
In and to a place, a people, a common history.
Even as a child when I was slurred in school –
Towel head, dot boy, camel jockey–
None of the abuse was precise: only Sikhs
Wear turbans, widows and young girls bindis,
Not one species of camel is indigenous to India...
If, as Simone Weil writes, to be rooted
Is the most important and least recognized need
Of the human soul, behold: I am an epiphyte.
I conjure sustenance from thin air and the smell
Of both camphor and meatloaf equally repel me.
I've worn a lungi pulled between my legs,
Done designer drugs while subwoofers throbbed,
Sipped masala chai steaming from a tin cup,
Driven a Dodge across the Verrazano in rush hour,
And always to some degree felt extraneous,
Like a meteorite happened upon bingo night.
This alien feeling, honed in aloneness to an edge,
Uses me to carve an appropriate mask each morning.
I'm still unsure what effect it has on my soul.

Misty Blue

Reared for the afternoon, the boutiques display
Furniture, fur-coated mannequins, defunct signs
From a passed time, as we stroll along Broadway,
Serene, until there's a mild censure, the saturnine
Response, a harsher rebuke, my defensive thrust,
And soon we two, nearly grown one, are at war,
Charged with anger that doesn't turn to lust
As it does in the movies. We stop at a parked car,
Oblivious to the passing faces, and try to rip free
From the gravity that holds us, verifying love
As an algorithm of hate, something guaranteed
To hurt. Drained, we turn. Then as if from above
Comes *Misty Blue*, a version Ella Fitzgerald sings.
The music, while it lasts, changes everything.

Notes

Samadhi, a Sanskrit word, refers to a state of deep absorption into the object of meditation, and the goal of many kinds of yoga. In Buddhism the term refers to any state of one-pointed concentration. In Hinduism it signifies the highest levels of mystical contemplation, in which the individual consciousness unifies with Godhead.

Wallace Stevens married Elsie Moll in 1909. Originally from Reading, Stevens' birthplace, she was considered a beauty so statuesque that she would later became the model for the Liberty-head dime and Liberty half-dollar.

Oviparity is the expulsion of undeveloped eggs rather than live young.

Vervain, or as it is more commonly known, Verbena, has also been called Juno's tears, Herb of the Cross, Pigeonweed, and Simpler's Joy. It was a Druidic sacred herb thought to treat depression and melancholia. It grows in waysides and waste places.

The 1911 fire at Coney Island was started when a worker accidentally kicked over a tub of hot tar used to caulk a leak in Hellgate, a boat ride through dimly lit caverns. The flames, fanned by the breeze, were unable to be quenched by the horse-drawn fire engines, and rapidly spread throughout the amusement park, Dreamland. A three-year old black-manned Nubian lion named Black Prince and a beloved bull elephant, Little Hip, were among the only casualties.

Haruspices were ancient Etruscan priests in who practiced divination by inspecting the entrails of animals. The Roman Senate held this mystical art in high regard and consulted haruspices before all important state decisions. A thaumaturge is a bringer of miracles.

The Triangulum galaxy, M33, is another a member of our Local Group of Galaxies, smaller than its neighbors Andromeda and the Milky Way but typical of spiral galaxies in the universe. "Instrumentality" is also indebted to Malcom Gladwell's article "The Young Garmentos," which first appeared in *The New Yorker*, for its descriptions of glove making.

The city of Bombay ("Bom bay" in Portuguese meant Good Bay) recently reverted back to its pre-colonial name, Mumbai (named after the many shrines dedicated to Mumbadevi, a Hindu goddess) in celebration of India's fifty year anniversary of gaining independence from British rule. Vasai, Ulhas, and Thane are the names of the rivers which surround Mumbai. *Bharathanatyam* is the oldest Indian dance form. Tradition has it that Brahama, moved by the entreaties of Indra and other devas for a pastime befitting the inhabitants of the celestial region, distilled the essence of the four Vedas and compounded them into this narrative dance form.

Sir Walter Raleigh wrote "The Nymph's Reply to the Shepherd" (1600) in response to Marlowe's "The Passionate Shepherd to his Love" (1599).

Heterophony was a term used by Plato to describe the simultaneous and often improvisatory dialogue between two or more performers (e.g., a singer and an instrumentalist) playing the same melody, creating aural texture.

Bhaja Govindam is one of the minor compositions of the Hindu poet/saint Adi Shankara (820 AD).

Bindis are derived from the Sanskrit word *bindu*, or dot. Generally made with vermilion powder and worn between the eyes by Hindu women, it is considered a symbol of the goddess Parvati, a source of female energy, and a traditional symbol of marriage. An epiphyte, or air plant, is a rootless plant that grows on another plant for support, though not for nourishment. A *lungi* is a brightly colored cloth made of cotton or silk that's worn as a loincloth by men in India and Pakistan. *Masala chai* is Indian spiced tea, made from cinnamon, cardamom, cloves, ginger, black pepper, lemongrass and mint. When it opened in 1964, the Verrazano Narrows Bridge was the world's largest suspension bridge. Unlike the Brooklyn Bridge, it has no poem addressed to it.

About the Author

Ravi Shankar was born in Washington DC, grew up in Manassas, Virginia, eventually matriculating at the University of Virginia and Columbia University. He is currently poet-in-residence at Central Connecticut State University and a founding editor of the internationally acclaimed online journal of the arts, Drunken Boat, <http://www.drunkenboat.com>. His poems have won a number of awards, including *Gulf Coast's* annual poetry prize. His critical work has previously appeared in Poets & Writers, Smartish Pace, The Iowa Review, and The AWP Writer's Chronicle. He reviews poetry for the Contemporary Poetry Review and is currently editing an anthology of South Asian, East Asian, and Middle Eastern poetry. Today you can find him living in the town of Chester, Connecticut. He does not play the sitar.